TORNADO!

THE STRONGEST WINDS ON EARTH

BY MIKE GRAF

Perfection Learning® CA

Cover Photo: Digital Stock
Inside Illustration: Michael A. Aspengren, Kay Ewald

About the Author

Mike Graf is a former elementary school teacher, a television weathercaster, and the author of several children's and teacher books including *Cave Story: An Underground Adventure, Thunder and Lightning, The Weather Report, National Parks Projects,* and *The World's Best Places.*

Mike has been into storms since he was a child. He loves to experience severe weather, safely from a distance! Mike hopes to go on a storm-chaser safari sometime in the near future.

Acknowledgments

I absolutely loved writing *Tornado! The Strongest Winds on Earth.* I have always been an overly curious person and into the weather. If I had grown up in the Midwest, I may have made the same mistake Tim made.

All the people portrayed in the story are based upon real people I have had the opportunity to meet. As a teacher and television weathercaster, I've been in the right settings to meet appropriate characters for *Tornado!*

I have had much help. In particular, I want to thank Jeff Slater of KAKE-TV Wichita, the National Weather Service, Dr. Mary Ann Cooper, Dan Graf of The Weather Channel, and the Wichita School District. All of you helped this story become more accurate and compelling.

I also want to thank my editor, Kathleen Mcfarren.

Image Credits: Art Today p. 8 (bottom); Bettmann/UPI p. 49; Lon Curtis p. 50 (top); Matt Dennis pp. 10, 33 (4th, 5th); Digital Stock pp. front cover, 3, 4–5, 11 (bottom), 12, 13, 17, 20, 25 (top), 29 (bottom), 36, 43, 45, 46, 47, 55, back cover; Library of Congress p. 28 (top); National Archives pp. 11 (top), 34 (top), 42; OAR/ER/National Severe Storms Laboratory pp. 8 (1st, 2nd, 3rd in cloud chart), 9, 23, 25 (bottom), 26, 28 (bottom), 29 (top), 31, 32, 33 (1st, 2nd, 3rd), 34 (bottom), 35, 39, 40, 50 (bottom), 51

Table of Contents

"This is a **tornado** tube," Tim Skinner said eagerly. He held up two one-liter bottles. They were attached with a small plastic tube. He wanted to show his classmates how to make a tornado—inside the bottles.

He was about to set the tube on the desk. But he lost his grip. And the whole gadget fell to the floor!

"Way to go, Funnel Cloud Boy!" Greg barked.

Several other students laughed.

Tim quickly picked up his tube and tried again. But there were equal amounts of water in each bottle. So when he shook it, nothing happened.

"Big tornado there," Greg mocked again.

Tim ignored Greg. He let the water drain from one bottle to the other. As soon as it did, he picked it up. And he shook it vigorously. Then he said, "Now watch this tornado!"

A huge funnel formed in the water. It drained from one bottle to the other.

"Hey! That's cool!" Greg called out.

"Let me try that!" several students said.

"Later," Mr. D said. "Very impressive, Tim. I think we'll make a whole science center with your report. I'll help you."

"That's not fair!" Greg yelled. "Why does he get—"

RING—RING—RING!

The recess bell interrupted Greg's protest.

"Hey, Tim," Mr. D said as Tim walked out the door. "Don't let Greg bug you. Okay?"

"Okay," Tim answered.

"I'll take care of it," explained Mr. D. "And—here. I thought you'd like to look at this right away."

Mr. D handed Tim his report on tornadoes.

Tim took the report outside. He flipped to the first page. It said

"A+. Nice job, Tim. This is great!
May I make a copy of this to show to future classes?"

Tim smiled. Then his best friend, Jill, walked up.

"Hey! It's Funnel Cloud Boy!" she teased.

Tim shook his head. "I really don't mind when *you* call me that. But Greg really bugs me."

"I know," Jill replied. She was kind of sorry she'd teased him. Quickly she added, "I really liked your report. Especially the tornado tube. That was cool. May I try it?"

"Sure. Why don't you stop by this weekend?"

The two headed to their next class.

Chapter 2

The next day, Tim visited Eric Loffman. Eric was a **meteorologist** at Wichita's KUSW-TV studios. Eric was finishing a map for his weathercast. The map was going to show that day's high temperatures.

Eric put 85 for south Wichita. Then he turned to Tim.

Severe Thunderstorms on a Satellite Loop

When the sun heats the ground during the day, the air becomes unstable. There is a layer of stable air called a *cap* in the atmosphere.

Energy builds up at the cap. Once energy breaks through the cap, clouds can grow up to 50,000 or 60,000 feet in height. Daylight heating and the cold air way above the ground cause this to happen.

Warm air from the ground keeps rising. It fuels the growth of the thunderstorm. Most severe thunderstorms and tornadoes occur in late afternoon or early evening. That's because they've been fueled by the sunshine and warm air all day long.

At any given moment, nearly 2,000 thunderstorms are in progress over the earth's surface. There are at least 100,000 thunderstorms yearly in the United States.

Thunderstorms produce strong gusts of cold wind or heavy rain and **hail.** Lightning usually occurs during a thunderstorm.

Sometimes, during a violent stage of a severe thunderstorm, a tornado forms.

A severe thunderstorm often appears in a V shape on a satellite photo. A storm with a tornado often has a hooked shape.

"I'm glad you're one of my **weather watchers,**" he said. "We really needed someone to report the weather from your part of town. And you do such a good job."

"My dad set up that weather station in our backyard," said Tim. "As soon as he did, we couldn't wait to report the temperatures to you. We're just happy you need it."

Tim had been visiting Eric every Thursday for over a month. But he was still in awe of the weather center. He glanced around. His eyes found the **cloud chart.** He focused on the different types of towering **cumulonimbus** clouds. He walked closer to study them.

Eric noticed Tim's interest. And he called him over to the weather computer. "Here are some severe **thunderstorms** on a satellite loop," he said. Eric's maps repeated themselves over and over. "Look at that massive thunderstorm grow into a V shape."

Stages of Thunderstorms

Thunderstorms have three stages. In the **cumulus** stage, the cloud is **updrafting.** The winds are moving up in the cloud. And it develops into a cumulonimbus cloud.

The mature stage of a thunderstorm has violent weather. **Updrafts** and **downdrafts** are side by side during this stage.

The shrinking stage of a thunderstorm has mostly downdrafts of air. These cause the storm to eventually dissipate.

Tim glanced back at the cloud chart. He wanted to take another look at a cumulonimbus cloud.

Cloud Chart

Clouds come in many shapes and sizes. Different kinds of clouds occur with different types of weather. You can use clouds to understand and forecast weather. There are four basic cloud types.

Cumulus

These are piled. They are formed by rising air currents. These clouds are fluffy. They usually occur during sunny weather. They may be filled with energy and continue to grow. When that happens, the air is very unstable.

Cirrus

These are curled. They are mostly made of ice crystals. These clouds are feathery streaks that float across the blue sky. Cirrus clouds tell us that a storm is coming.

Cumulonimbus

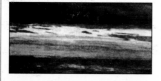

These are very dense. They bring thunderstorms. The storms can include heavy rain, hail, lightning, and thunder. And they can even include tornadoes. These clouds have a strong vertical development and huge cauliflower-like shapes. They often have an anvil shape at the top.

Stratus

These are sheetlike or layered. They are a stable layer of clouds. These clouds look flat. They may produce rain. But it is a slow drizzle rather than a violent, short-lived thunderstorm.

"Those 60,000-feet-tall puppies can produce tornadoes," Eric said. "Here. Let me show you something."

Eric pulled out a videotape from his drawer. The label said "Tornadoes '96." Eric inserted the tape and pressed play.

A **funnel cloud** drifted across the screen. It touched the ground. And it kicked up a whirlwind of dust and debris.

Tornado Formation

The winds far above the ground are called the *jet stream*. They are the key to tornado formation. *Shearing* winds must be in the jet. This means that the winds above are changing direction with height.

Winds from the southeast usually contain moist air. When they hit cool, dry winds from the southwest, **rotation** starts. Rotation inside a thunderstorm is the first sign of a developing tornado.

The photographers popped in and out of the picture. They were squealing with delight. Witnessing a tornado and capturing it on film was sheer bliss for them.

One of the photographers called out, "Oh, my! Look at that thing. It's beautiful!"

The other added, "Tornado on the ground! Tornado on the ground!"

"That's nothing," Eric explained. "Maybe just an F0 or an F1 tornado."

Eric fast-forwarded the tape to the next storm.

"Now," he said. "Take a look at *this* baby!"

A huge twister tore through an Oklahoma town. Dust and debris were being blown everywhere.

"Watch this. That's a car being tossed in the air! And look— there goes a truck!"

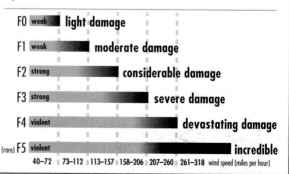

Fujita Scale

The **Fujita Scale** measures wind damage in tornadoes. The scale rates tornadoes by how much damage they caused. All tornadoes are assigned a single number from this scale.

F0 weak	light damage	
F1 weak	moderate damage	
F2 strong	considerable damage	
F3 strong	severe damage	
F4 violent	devastating damage	
(rare) F5 violent	incredible	

40–72 73–112 113–157 158–206 207–260 261–318 wind speed (miles per hour)

Stages of a Tornado

Tornadoes can be very hard to predict. The length of a tornado's cycle is even more unpredictable.

However, tornadoes do seem to have a definite life cycle. The stages of a tornado are

Stage 1: Dust Whirl

Stage 2: Organization

Stage 3: Mature

Stage 4: Shrinking

Stage 5: Decaying

A funnel cloud extends toward the ground during the dust-whirl stage. That is the beginning of the tornado.

If the funnel cloud reaches the ground, it moves into the organization stage.

The funnel reaches its maximum width and is perpendicular to the ground. Then it is a mature tornado. That is the third stage.

The tornado begins to scatter and cover a wide span. That means it has entered the shrinking stage.

Finally, in the decaying stage, the tornado has almost completely dissolved. During this stage, it is small and thin. And it seems to crawl back into the sky.

The twister was tossing cars as if they were matchboxes. But it was doing so much more. It was destroying everything in its path.

"That's a tornado!" Eric exclaimed. "And right there in Oklahoma. That's the heart of **Tornado Alley.**"

Eric walked back to his computer. And Tim watched more of the video.

The next storm Tim saw was not a tornado. It was a thunderstorm. It dropped hailstones the size of baseballs across a field in Nebraska. Those who were filming it had their windshield smashed by the ice.

Tim glanced over his shoulder. Eric was getting his maps ready for the next weathercast. He was working on one for Wichita and all of southeast Kansas.

Eric picked up his cut-and-paste pen. He pushed it down on the computer mat. And he traced a square around a large cloud.

Eric lifted the cloud up to a blank page. And he switched pages to the southeast Kansas map. He pasted the cloud there. Then Eric added lightning and tornado symbols to the map.

Tim knew what that meant. Tomorrow was going to be a crazy weather day. It would be a weather watcher's dream day.

Tim turned back to the tape. The latest twister on the video had *roped out.* That meant that the tornado was just about over. The long, thin rope of a funnel snaked across the horizon. It was a beautiful sight.

Eric tapped Tim on the shoulder.

"C'mon. It's showtime," Eric said.

They walked into the studio. Tim saw the large green weather wall.

The Chroma-Key

The Chroma-Key is an important part of television technology. It takes the color green or blue and replaces it with images. During the weather report, the images are likely to be weather maps.

As a TV viewer, you would see the maps. But you would not see the color.

A weathercaster has to choose his or her clothing carefully. He or she cannot wear an item of clothing that's the same color as the Chroma-Key. If the weathercaster does, that item of clothing will be invisible to the viewer.

"I still can't figure something out," Tim said. "How do you always find the right place to point to?" Tim remembered giving a pretend weather report in front of the wall. And it hadn't been easy!

"Wait till you're a weatherman," Eric replied. "Then you'll get used to the Chroma-Key."

Eric took his place on the set. And Tim watched the live newscast.

Lynn, the anchorwoman, described the flooding in Ohio and Indiana. TV monitors in the studio showed videos of people affected by the flood.

Some were stranded on top of their homes with floodwaters all around. A car floated down a roadway. Another clip showed a mailman sloshing through knee-deep water.

Lynn finished the story by saying, "There's no flooding here. But meteorologist Eric Loffman says we do have a chance of some severe weather. He'll be right back with your forecast."

"Hey, Tim!" Lynn said during the commercial. "Nice to see you again. How are you?"

"Fine, thanks. It's nice to see you too."

The cameraman called out, "Ten seconds, Eric!"

Eric quickly adjusted his microphone. He straightened his tie. Then he looked at the camera and smiled.

The cameraman said, "5—4—3..."

"Looks like a fairly calm night," Eric began. He showed a mostly blank **radar** map with a few specks of green. "Radar is only picking up a few distant showers now. But tomorrow—look out!"

Eric's maps switched. The new one showed all the plains.

"This front here will combine with a surge of warm, moist air from the **Gulf of Mexico.** These **air masses** will meet with drier air coming from the west."

Eric's map now had a series of fronts and arrows drawn on it.

"All this will meet right over our area," he said.

Eric's map switched again. This one showed a close-up of southern Kansas, including Wichita.

"About mid-afternoon tomorrow. That's when we'll really have to watch out!"

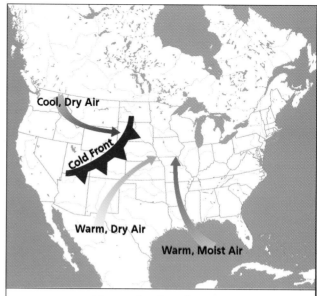

Tornado Conditions

Certain conditions are needed for a tornado to occur. First, there needs to be dry air from the southwest. The leading edge of the dry air is called the **dry line.** This air meets up with warm air from the Gulf of Mexico. Also, a **cold front** typically drops down out of the north. These three air masses hit one another, or *collide*.

Thunderstorms develop along the dry line. The dry line is a boundary between very moist and very dry air. When these air masses meet, instability can explode.

Those are the conditions necessary for a tornado. They happen most often on the plains.

Chapter 3

Tim's alarm rang at six o'clock. He jumped out of bed, walked to the window, and checked the clouds. The sky was clear. But he knew it wouldn't be for long.

He thought about Eric's words:

"About mid-afternoon tomorrow. That's when we'll really have to watch out!"

Tim couldn't wait for it to happen!

I hope it happens at lunchtime, he thought. I can be outside to see the clouds. And anything that might come out of them!

Tim took out his maps of the U.S. They were covered in plastic that he could write on.

With an erasable pen, he outlined Oklahoma, Nebraska, and Kansas. Tim drew large arrows. They showed dry air coming from the west. And moist air coming up from the Gulf of Mexico.

Then Tim drew another line. It went from Scottsbluff, Nebraska, to Denver, Colorado, and down to Albuquerque, New Mexico. He drew triangles pointing east from that line. This showed that the cold front was moving toward Kansas.

Tim knew from Eric's weather report that the storm had dropped golf ball-sized hail yesterday. Hail had fallen in northwest Nebraska and eastern Colorado. And a few funnel clouds had been spotted. But none had touched down and become tornadoes.

Tim drew on his other map. He drew the cold front much farther east and the warm-air arrows farther north. This was where the air masses were expected to be at mid-afternoon today. Right over Wichita!

Tim put a big **X** by Wichita. He posted the two maps on his wall. Then he gave a pretend weather report to Rainbow, his cat.

"We will have severe weather today. Look out, Wichita! This storm will drop down and hit warm air from the Gulf of Mexico. Thunderstorms will explode this afternoon when the warm, cool, and dry air meet over Kansas!"

Tim screamed out his last sentence. And Rainbow ran for cover. Tim noticed her tail sticking out from under his bed.

Homemade Weather Station

Home or school weather stations can be carefully constructed out of plywood.

These instruments can be added to the shelter:

- ➤ thermometer
- ➤ **barometer**
- ➤ rain gauge
- ➤ cloud chart
- ➤ **wind vane**
- ➤ anemometer
- ➤ **hygrometer**

Information gathered at home weather stations is often used by local media or even the National Weather Service.

Tim threw on his jacket and shoes and went outside. It was time to check his weather station.

He walked out to the white wooden box. Inside was a **maximum/minimum thermometer.** It checked the high and low temperatures. Outside was a **rain gauge.** There was also an **anemometer** for the wind speed and a **wind sock** to check the wind direction.

Tim opened the flap that protected the thermometer from the sun.

Tim read the thermometer. It was very warm for an April morning. It was 68 degrees. And the low the night before had been 65.

Maximum/Minimum Thermometer

Temperature measures the speed of air molecules. The faster the molecules move, the higher the temperature.

A maximum/minimum thermometer uses mercury and magnet strips to determine the different temperatures. Mercury pushes the magnets to the extreme low or high temperature for the day. Then it moves back, leaving the magnets in place until they are reset. The position of the magnets tells the high and low temperatures of the day.

The thermometer is shaped like a U. This creates the scale on the low side and the scale on the high side. The low scale is read from the top down. But the high scale is read from the bottom up. Just like a regular thermometer.

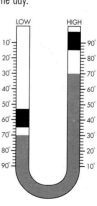

15

According to the anemometer and the wind sock, the wind was blowing lightly now. It was coming from the southeast at 6 miles per hour.

Only a few small cumulus clouds were in the distant, hazy sky. Tim scribbled all this information on scratch paper. Then he went inside to write it on his weather chart.

Tim's Weather Chart

Date	High	Low	Barometer	Wind Direction and Speed
April 22	75	45	30.00	NW 12
April 23	76	52	29.95	SW 5
April 24	84	60	29.78	SW 20
April 25	85	63	29.70	S 22
April 26		65	29.63	S 18

Tim ran downstairs.

First, he filled Rainbow's food dish. Rainbow knew the sound of food pouring into her dish. In a flash, she was downstairs, rubbing up against Tim's leg. Her thundering purr brightened Tim's mood.

"I want you to stay inside today," Tim warned. "There's a huge storm coming."

Rainbow answered with a meow and a flick of her tail. Then she lowered her head into her bowl.

Tim fixed himself a bowl of cereal. And the two friends happily ate their breakfast.

Tim's mom wandered into the kitchen. "Good morning," she said brightly.

"Good morning, Mom."

"In a hurry?" she asked.

"I'm late," Tim said.

"Lovely milk mustache, Tim."

Tim smiled. And his mom handed him his lunch bag.

"Don't forget to go to the office at lunchtime," she said. "You need to take your medicine. I know you're feeling better. But remember last time? You have to finish the medicine so you won't get sick again. Promise you won't forget."

"I promise."

But Tim's mind was on the storm. He threw his lunch into his backpack.

"Bye, Mom," he said. "This is really going to be a great day!"

"I hope so," his mom said. She kissed him on the cheek. And Tim dashed out the door.

Maybe I'll finally get to see a real tornado! he thought.

He checked the clouds. Towering cumulus clouds were starting to swell in the sky. And it was only eight o'clock in the morning.

Tim checked the thermometer dangling from his jacket. It was 70 degrees now. He knew that the temperature would drop later.

Early Signs of a Tornado

Major tornadoes come from huge cumulonimbus clouds. Thunderstorms can have wall clouds that fall below the bottom of the cumulonimbus clouds.

Rotation starts in a wall cloud. That's where severe weather can occur—including tornadoes.

Check for wall clouds and rotation inside a large, growing cumulonimbus cloud. That way, you can see if a tornado is forming.

Chapter 4

Jill was waiting for Tim on her porch. She did so every day.

"Hi, Tim," she called out as he walked up.

Tim continued to look at the sky. Jill stared at him for a few seconds. Finally, she said, "HELLO!"

Tim didn't respond.

Jill fell into step with Tim. "Did you even see me?" she asked.

Tim finally glanced in her direction. He smiled and said, "Hello."

"So what's going on up there?" Jill asked. "Is it going to be as bad as Eric Loffman said?"

"We're going to find out what it means to live in Tornado Alley," he replied.

"What does that mean?"

"It means it's going to be *bad* today."

Jill glanced up curiously at the darkening sky.

Tim continued. "It means we live smack-dab in the middle of where the most powerful storms in the world occur. Tornadoes. Right here."

Jill and Tim hurried off to school. They walked under the many trees on Elm Street. Most of the homes there were over 50 years old.

Tornado Alley

In the U.S., tornadoes are most likely to occur in the central and north-central regions. But many forecasters call Kansas, Missouri, Oklahoma, and Texas "Tornado Alley."

Tornado Alley's most active period is from March through July. That's when conditions are just right for tornadoes.

Worldwide, Tornado Alley reports the most severe and the largest number of tornadoes. About 700 tornadoes occur yearly in this region.

Conditions for tornadoes come together here like nowhere else in the world. Warm, moist air comes up from the Gulf of Mexico. Drier air comes from the desert southwest. Fronts move in from the west and northwest with cooler air.

The different types of air cause a change in wind direction. And there are no mountains over the plains to alter any of these air currents.

Tim ran his hand along Mr. Johnson's metal fence. He and Jill both smiled at the familiar sign—

"Warning! This dog bites!"

Tim and Jill looked at each other. "Bet I can keep my hand here longer than you," Tim said.

"Bet not," Jill replied.

Jill and Tim grabbed the top of the

fence. Tim rattled it and called out, "Here, Fang! Here, Fang!"

The big Doberman dashed out from the backyard. Jill and Tim kept their hands on the fence. They dared each other to see who was braver. The Doberman hurled himself against the fence. He barked and growled, baring his teeth.

The two yanked their hands away. Just in time!

Tim laughed, "What are ya gonna do now, Fang?"

"Yeah, Fang!" Jill added.

Jill and Tim laughed again and headed off to school.

Finally, they reached Elm Street Middle School. Students streamed off the big yellow buses.

Jill poked her elbow into Tim. She said, "Hey, Tim. Sorry I called you Funnel Cloud Boy yesterday."

Tim stopped and looked at Jill. Then he stared back up at the sky. The clouds were darkening and continuing to grow. Soon the sunshine would be completely gone.

"We'd better get to class," Tim said. Then he smiled. "That nickname may really ring true before this day is out."

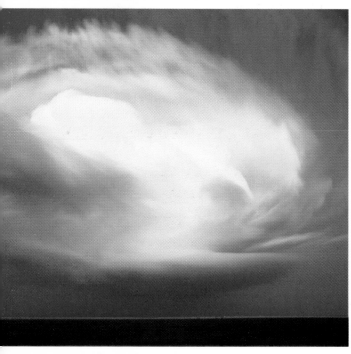

Chapter 5

The morning bell rang. And all the kids filed in.

Mr. D greeted his students. "Good morning. Nice to see all of you today."

"Good morning," they replied.

Once the class was seated, Mr. D got serious.

"Class, we'll go over your assignment in a little bit. But first, we need to talk about something."

Tim looked outside. His heart jumped. A large cumulonimbus cloud was exploding in height. It was taking on a cauliflower-like shape at the top. Rotation, he knew, could start soon.

Mr. D went on. "The other teachers and I were talking before school. We are going to have severe weather today."

Tim raised his hand.

"Yes?" said Mr. D.

"And tornadoes," replied Tim.

"Right, Funnel Cloud Boy," Greg sneered.

A few students laughed.

Mr. D looked sternly at Greg. Greg sat up and pressed his lips into a line.

Just then, a crackling sound came over the loudspeaker.

"Good morning, ladies and gentlemen. This is your principal, Mrs. Hamlett. I have just received word—there are some severe storms about an hour southwest of Wichita.

"We need to be prepared for the possibility of severe weather. We will announce a practice drill in a few moments.

"We'll do a drop drill. Remember what can hurt us—broken glass and falling objects. When the drop drill bell rings, go into the hallway. Get against the wall. Sit down cross-legged. And bend down and protect your head."

RING. RING. RING. RING.

The class walked out the door quickly. They'd had many drop drills. But it seemed more serious today.

The students walked straight to their assigned places in the hall. They immediately sat down and covered their heads.

Mr. D made sure everyone was out of the class and properly dropped. Then he took a quick roll call. He kept glancing at the windows.

"Listen, everyone," he announced. "This is serious. I need to make sure we are all okay. Just as I'd do during the real thing."

Tim pulled out his **weather radio.** He kept the volume low and held it up to his ear. This is what he heard:

"This is the National Weather Service. A line of severe storms is moving northeast into southern Kansas. Severe weather can be expected. This includes thunderstorms, large hail, and numerous tornadoes.

"Wichita, Dodge City, and all surrounding areas need to be on special alert. A *tornado watch* has been issued for south central Kansas. This includes Sedgwick, Butler, Kingman, Pratt, Barber, Harper, and Sumner counties. This watch is in effect from 10 A.M. until 4 P.M. today.

"A *tornado watch* means that conditions are right for the development of a tornado in or close to this watch area."

Weather Radio

Weather radios receive continuous broadcasts from the National Weather Service. Broadcasts are updated 24 hours a day, 7 days a week.

Some of the radios have a special alert feature. This will sound an alarm if the National Weather Service issues a watch or warning.

Tim's heart raced. The storm was coming!

Jill caught Tim's attention. She knew he was listening to his weather radio. She mouthed, "Is everything okay?"

"No," Tim shook his head.

Watches and Warnings

The National Weather Service provides information on weather. And they keep the public informed about weather hazards. Here are some examples of hazardous weather.

- tornadoes
- severe thunderstorms
- hail
- winter storms
- dense fog
- dust or sand storms
- freezing rain
- blizzards
- high winds
- floods
- dam breaks

A *watch* lets people know that a weather hazard could happen. Once a watch is issued, people need to be ready to take action.

A *warning* lets people know that a particular weather hazard is happening. Once a warning has been issued, people must act quickly. Quick action is needed to protect themselves and their property.

During severe weather, it is important to stay alert. Especially to the watches and warnings issued by the nearest weather center.

Local television and radio stations use National Weather Service watches and warnings to alert the public.

Mr. D's feet tapped Tim's feet. Mr. D knelt down. "How's it looking Tim?" he asked. And he held his ear to the weather radio too.

The announcer spoke.

"The area between Wichita and Dodge City is at risk. The energy of the storm will be focused in this region. These storms are already causing problems to the southwest. As the day unfolds, the potential for damaging weather will increase."

Tim and Mr. D looked at each other.
"It's going to be one of those days," Mr. D said.
"Yep," replied Tim.

Meanwhile, Eric Loffman was tracking the weather at the studio. He'd come to work early that day. He and Sharon, the morning meteorologist, would cover the storm together.

"What do you think, Sharon?" Eric asked.

"I've been checking the conditions all morning," she said. "We already have large cumulonimbus clouds. **Supercell storms** are developing along the dry line. I think we're going to have tornadoes."

"I agree," Eric said.

"I'll get a Tornado Watch map ready," Sharon said.

Gary, the news director, walked into the weather center.

"Look at this!" Eric said.

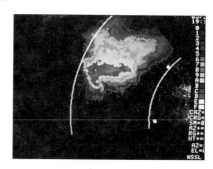

Eric brought up a radar loop on his computer. It showed a line of red and orange moving toward Wichita.

"There are the thundershowers. And they're getting larger. There are even some purple areas showing up on radar. That means there are already severe storms with heavy rain."

"Better get ready, guys," Gary said. "We're on the air in ten minutes."

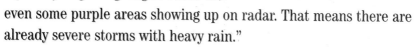

Raindrop Size

There are strong drafts of air inside a large cumulonimbus cloud. This causes raindrops to sometimes be held up, or suspended, in the air. They come together with other drops until they are heavy enough to fall to the ground. Larger thunderstorms often produce huge raindrops.

Follow these steps to measure the raindrops from a thundershower.

1. Put one inch of flour into a tin pan.
2. Shake the pan gently until the flour is smooth and even.
3. Put the pan out in the rain.
4. Let a few drops hit the flour. Then bring the pan inside.
5. Measure the size of the drops.

Repeat this experiment on different rainy days. Compare the size of the drops. Remember, bigger raindrops come from larger clouds.

Back at Elm Street Middle School, the loudspeaker crackled.

"Ladies and gentlemen, the drop drill is over. You may return to your rooms. If we have another drop drill today, it will be the real thing. Please be prepared to protect yourselves. We want you all to be safe. Thank you for your cooperation."

Tim's class got up and walked back to their classroom.

Huge splats of rain began smacking against the windows.

The rain fell harder. The drops were being driven by gusts of wind. The students kept glancing at the windows. It was getting darker.

I wish I could check the whole sky now, Tim thought.

Suddenly, the lights in the classroom flickered on and off. Lightning flashed outside.

"1, 2, 3, 4, 5. 1, 2, 3, 4, 5," Tim counted aloud. Then came a loud KA-BOOM of thunder.

Without thinking, Jill ducked and protected her head. So did many of the other students.

"It's about two miles away!" Tim exclaimed.

"There goes Funnel Cloud Boy again," Greg mocked. "He thinks he knows everything."

"Shut up. He knows what he's talking about," Jill fought back. She glanced at Tim to say, "Sorry." And she shrugged.

The Flash-to-Bang Method

Measuring lightning's distance is easy if you use the Flash-to-Bang Method.

Once you see a flash, start counting. When you hear thunder, stop counting.

If you get to 5, the lightning is 1 mile away. If you get to 10, it is 2 miles. Every 5 seconds count as a mile.

"That's enough," said Mr. D. "There will be no more teasing from anyone. Period."

The rain came down harder and harder. Then it started pounding on the roof. That's when everyone realized it had turned to hail!

The hail got harder, louder, and bigger. Soon it was the size of golf balls.

The students ran to the window to watch nature's show. It looked like hundreds of golf balls were being tossed down from the sky. And they were pounding the playground. The roar of the hail on the roof was deafening.

The clouds were dark black. There were pouches in some of the clouds.

"**Mammatus clouds.** That means the clouds could be rotating," Tim mumbled. He wanted to remember every bit of this storm.

I wish I had my camera, he thought. I'd love to show this to Eric.

"Everyone back to your seats now!" Mr. D demanded.

"Do we have to?" whined several students.

"I want to watch!" cried others.

But there was no changing his mind. Mr. D knew it wasn't safe to stand near the windows. Not during a hailstorm.

The class settled back into their seats. The hailstorm seemed to let up a bit.

Just then—CRASH! A large chunk of ice broke through the window. It slid across the floor.

Several students ran to grab it.

"Wait!" Tim exclaimed. "We can freeze it. Then we can slice it open later and check the layers. Don't let it melt."

Mr. D walked over to take the baseball-sized hailstone. And two more large balls of ice broke through another part of the window.

"Arrrghh!" several students screamed. They quickly tried to dodge flying ice and glass.

"Owwww! It hit me!" Jill cried.

"Duck and cover!" Mr. D yelled. There was panic in his voice.

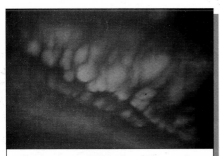

Mammatus Clouds and Rotation

Mammatus clouds can be part of a cumulunimbus cloud. They have pouches near the bottom of them. They are often considered warning clouds. They indicate that rotation has started in the cloud. And that it might lead to a tornado.

Strong thunderstorms need rotation inside to develop funnel clouds and tornadoes. Mammatus clouds show that the thundercloud has started to *downdraft*. This means it is bringing wet air down. And then it is warming it up in an updraft.

This action can begin to rotate the thunderstorm.

The whole class reacted at once. They dropped to the floor. And they put their heads under their desks.

Mr. D quickly checked the room. Jill was holding her arm.

"Are you hurt?" Mr. D asked.

"I don't think so." She looked up. Her arm was red. But she wasn't bleeding.

Mr. D stood up and gave further directions.

"Get up. Slide your desks away from the window. Then get under them again and protect your heads. Now!"

The class immediately followed his command. As Tim was pushing his desk toward the wall, he looked over at Jill. "Are you okay?" he asked.

"I'm fine," she mouthed.

The school's loudspeaker crackled to life again. The class knew what this meant. The principal said—

"Ladies and gentlemen! Please get into the hallway right now. This is not a practice drill. The hail has broken windows all over the school. Get into the hallways. And duck and cover immediately!"

Chapter 6

Eric Loffman watched Sharon. She was doing the first break into regular TV programming. She reported—

"This growing thunderstorm is dropping large hail on the Wichita area. It is starting to show signs of rotation. Tornadoes are likely with this storm—soon."

Gary walked over to Eric. He said, "I want you to go out live toward south Wichita. I need you to cover the storm."

"We can't," answered Eric. "It wouldn't be safe. There are lightning strikes all over the place. I don't think we should take that live truck out anywhere. Not with our live antenna sticking up."

When the hail ended at the school, the power was almost totally out. Luckily, the school had an emergency generator. So they had some electricity. And the principal was still able to use the loudspeaker—

Lightning Rods

A **lightning rod** is a device used for keeping lightning away from buildings. Benjamin Franklin was the first person to suggest using the lightning rod.

Lightning rods attract strokes of lightning to the rod itself. This keeps lightning from hitting other parts of the ground or building.

The lightning rod only works in the final part of the lightning stroke's path to the earth. It cannot break up an entire thundercloud. It only reworks the lightning's path.

A lightning rod system has three main parts:

1. The rods on the roof of a building
2. The wires that connect the rods together
3. The wires that run down the sides of the house or building to the ground

"Students and teachers, the hail has let up now. So the drop drill is over for the time being. However, all students should be prepared to take cover at any moment. Our office will closely watch the storm."

The students returned to their classes.

In his room, Mr. D swept up the broken glass.

The students finished pushing their desks close to the inside wall.

Tim looked outside. The clouds were a deep, dark—almost purplish—gray. The winds howled through the trees and hallways. And huge raindrops continued to pelt against the glass.

It was nearly dark in the classroom. The candle Mr. D lit kept blowing out. A draft whistled through the broken window.

Mr. D had everyone sit down on the carpet. Then he went to the freezer and pulled out the hailstone.

"Pretty big, huh? Do you know how this was formed?"

Everyone looked right at Tim. Slowly, he raised his hand.

"Come up here, Tim," encouraged Mr. D. "Tell us what you know."

Tim walked up to the blackboard. Mr. D turned on a flashlight. That way, the students could see what Tim was drawing.

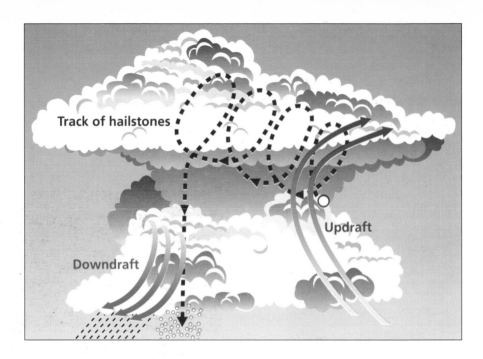

Track of hailstones

Updraft

Downdraft

Tim drew a large cumulonimbus cloud. Then he said, "Inside this cloud are a lot of raindrops. And a lot of wind. The raindrops try to fall out. But they get caught up in wind drafts.

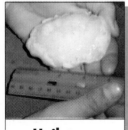

"If the raindrop is blown up to a high, cold part of the cloud, it's coated with a layer of ice. If the storm is super powerful, like the one we are having, this can happen over and over. Until the hailstone is finally heavy enough to leave the cloud."

Hailstone Classifications

Name	Size
Pea	0.25"
Penny	0.75"
Quarter	1.00"
Half Dollar	1.25"
Golf Ball	1.75"
Tennis Ball	2.50"
Baseball	2.75"
Grapefruit	4.00"

Hailstone Facts

- Hail is dangerous! In 1953, hailstones as large as golf balls fell in Alberta, Canada. They covered an area of 140 miles (225 km) by 5 miles (8 km). They killed thousands of birds.

- The largest single hailstone to fall to the ground was recorded at Coffeyville, Kansas. It fell on September 3, 1970. It weighed 1.67 pounds (750 g). And it had a diameter of 17.5 inches!

Tim held up the hailstone. "We can learn something from the number of layers in this. That tells us how many times it cycled through the cloud."

"Cool," Greg said. "Can I hold the hail?"

"Sure," Tim said. He handed Greg the piece of ice.

"Man, that's cold!" Greg commented. Then he started passing it around the room.

At the TV studio, Eric glanced at the most recent **satellite picture.** It showed a large cluster of clouds forming into a V shape. The most vicious thunderheads were in the tip of the V. And they were rolling into Wichita.

The phone rang. Eric picked it up. "Weather, Eric Loffman."

It was a storm-chaser friend. He had a report for Eric.

Eric repeated his friend's information.

"Another one is forming a couple of miles south . . . What's its movement? Yes . . . Uh-huh. That big! Wow! We will definitely report that. Thanks for calling. And stay safe out there!"

Eric walked into Gary's office.

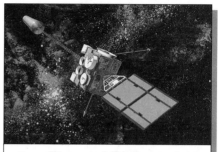

Satellite and Radar Loops

Meteorologists use special satellites to gauge the size of raindrops, hail, and dust. These satellites are connected to weather computers.

The computers send out signals. The signals bounce off rain, hail, and dust. Then they bounce back.

The signal is interpreted. The strength of the signal tells the size of the particle. It also tells how far away it is. Larger drops give off stronger signals. They show up as red and orange colors. Smaller drops are shown in green.

Doppler radar can detect rotation. But it cannot confirm whether a tornado is on the ground. That's why spotters on the ground are still needed.

"Sharon needs to stay on TV continually now," Eric said. "So she can report everything the storm does. A large tornado is touching down just south of town. Its path will take it right toward the Elm Street subdivision. That's near the middle school.

"I'm going to head over there! I don't mean with the live truck. But with a camera crew. Sharon and I will keep in touch over the **ham radio.**"

Gary responded, "We'll be on air immediately. You be careful!"

The production crew gathered equipment. Cameras, microphones, and lights were loaded in the van.

While waiting, Eric watched the beginning of Sharon's live news. She put up a map of the Wichita area. It showed the new tornado. Sharon added a line to the map. She said, "This is where the twister is moving. Right into south Wichita."

Gary came up to Eric. He said, "They're waiting for you outside."

"I hope this works out," replied Eric nervously.

"Me too," Gary added.

Eric climbed into the KUSW-TV van. The van sped toward the darkest part of the sky. It was 11:30 in the morning.

"You're sure you know what you're doing?" asked the driver.

"We'll only go as far as it is safe," said Eric. He knew that the fate of this crew rested on his shoulders.

Storm Chasing

Storm chasers follow severe weather. Some storm chasers photograph severe weather. Others want to study storms. Some people chase storms as a hobby.

Storm chasing is dangerous. So chasers use special equipment.

Warren Faidley, a well-known tornado chaser, uses a vehicle called "Shadow Chaser." It's a normal sport-utility vehicle, such as a Ford Explorer. But it has been turned into a portable weather center. His car has

- A front-mounted video camera. It can tape through the windshield.

- Several radios and CB scanners.

- A long-range cellular phone. It can be hooked up to a computer and access the World Wide Web.

- A complete weather center.

- Security and safety equipment.

There are 100,000 thunderstorms expected each year. But only about 1,000 of them produce tornadoes. Many of these happen at night. Or they are hidden by rain, hail, debris, and dust. Storm chasers have to be patient and persistent!

Tornado Movement

Tornadoes normally move from the southwest to northeast. However, they can be unpredictable. And they must be constantly monitored.

Most tornadoes are in the **rain-free base** of the cloud. This is the updraft area of the storm. It is usually on the southwest side of the cloud that is moving northeast.

Before the tornado hits, many thunderstorms often have a moment of calm. Rain and hail stop. At this time, the tornado is usually visible. But it can be hidden. So people may not see it coming.

"I'll keep calling Sharon," he added. "And I'll keep a close watch on the tornado."

At the school, rain still pelted the windows. The trees nearby were bending over and snapping like toothpicks.

Mr. D walked back to the freezer. He put the hailstone back.

"We can check the layers later," he said.

Tim thought he heard a train running down tracks. But he knew that the tracks were on the other side of town. His heart skipped a beat.

That's right, he thought. That's the sound of an approaching tornado! It's similar to the roar of a train, or an airplane, or even a waterfall.

The roar was getting louder. The bottom layer of clouds whirled around. It almost looked like a carnival carousel rotating in the sky.

Tim watched closely. He knew that the carousel shape was the result of a **mesocyclone.**

It's almost here! he thought.

"Ladies and gentleman!" announced the principal. "It's the real thing this time!"

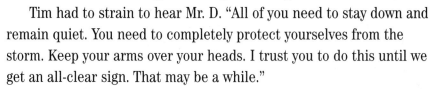

Chapter 7

"Everyone into the halls!" Mrs. Hamlett proclaimed. "A tornado is approaching our school!"

Students jumped out of their seats and moved quickly.

Mr. D warned, "Make sure your whole head is covered."

Every student got up against the wall, bent down. They put their arms over their heads. All was quiet. They all waited nervously.

The **tornado warning** sirens began wailing.

Tim had to strain to hear Mr. D. "All of you need to stay down and remain quiet. You need to completely protect yourselves from the storm. Keep your arms over your heads. I trust you to do this until we get an all-clear sign. That may be a while."

Mr. D looked down the hall and through the window. Trees and bushes blew across the playground. Fence posts were flying about. Sheets of rain blew sideways across the blacktop. It was dark and gray.

In the distance, Mr. D briefly saw the funnel cloud dance across the sky. It tore up trees, shrubs, and houses.

He said, "I have to protect myself now. Please stay quiet. I need to hear what is going on."

Mr. D sat down and protected his head. And a tree branch slammed against the door.

Tim tried to see out. But he couldn't. He glanced at his watch— 12:10 P.M. Just as Eric had predicted.

"Oh, no!" Tim suddenly remembered. "My medicine!"

I've got to get to the office, he thought. I promised Mom.

It was only about a 50-foot dash from one hallway to the other. He was one of the fastest runners in the school. So it would only take a few seconds.

Tim quietly stood up and dashed down the hall.

"Tim!" shouted Mr. D—just as the hallway door closed behind him.

Did you know?

Tornadoes move across land at about 30 mph. Some can spin in place. And others move as fast as 70 mph.

Measuring Wind Speed

There is no known way to measure the exact wind speed from a tornado. Scientists are trying to develop methods. But tornadoes don't travel right over wind instruments. And even if they did, the instruments would be damaged.

The Fujita Scale was developed to estimate wind speed. The estimate is based on post-tornado damage.

The fastest wind ever estimated in a tornado was 286 miles per hour. This was recorded on April 2, 1925, in Wichita Falls, Texas.

The Beaufort Scale measures the force of wind. Sir Francis Beaufort designed this scale in the 1850s. It was intended for use at sea. However, the scale has been adapted for land use. It is still used today.

The strongest wind ever recorded was 230 miles per hour! This was at the summit of Mount Washington, New Hampshire. It happened April 12, 1934.

The Beaufort Scale

Force	Speed per hour (in miles)	Description	Effect
1	1–3	light air	smoke slightly bent
2	4–6	light breeze	leaves rustle
3	7–10	gentle breeze	leaves move
4	11–16	moderate breeze	small branches move
5	17–21	fresh breeze	small trees sway
6	22–27	strong breeze	large branches move
7	28–33	near gale	whole trees sway
8	34–40	gale	twigs break off
9	41–47	strong gale	roofs damaged
10	48–55	storm	trees uprooted
11	56–63	violent storm	widespread damage
12	64+	hurricane	destruction

Tim stepped outside. For a second, Tim thought about turning around. But then he decided he could make it back before anyone knew he was gone.

He covered his head with his jacket. Once out in the open, he saw sheets of rain. And there were tree branches flying everywhere. Tim imagined a giant clearing his neighborhood with a huge leaf blower.

Tim ran toward the office. He struggled to get into the other hallway. Suddenly, a gust of wind knocked him down. He grabbed a pole and tried to hold himself up.

Tim heard the faint sound of the loudspeaker—

"Ladies and gentleman! A tornado has touched down near Elm Street—just a few blocks south of the school. This is a very dangerous situation. Please stay down. Protect yourselves until we get an all-clear signal."

Tim panicked. Elm Street! His neighborhood! His house!

Tim gripped the pole and stuck his head out into the storm. Rain hit his face. Through squinting eyes, he saw a funnel. It looked like a giant cattail hanging in the sky.

Rainbow! Tim thought. I forgot to close her cat door. What if she went outside?

Tim pulled out his weather radio. But it was impossible to hear anything. Out of the corner of his eye, he saw a huge cloud of dust and debris. It was being picked up near the bottom of the funnel.

"A tornado," Tim said. "I'm finally experiencing a real tornado!"

Tim suddenly wished that Eric, Jill, or his mom were there with him—or Greg—or maybe even his whole class!

For a few brief seconds, Tim saw the whole tornado. It was destroying everything in its path.

"Rainbow! My house!" Tim cried. "I've got to get out of here!"

Without thinking, Tim took off running. He ran through the gate at the school's parking lot. He ran right down Elm Street. He was headed straight for his house—and the tornado!

"Rainbow!" Tim screamed. "I'm coming!"

But running toward a tornado is very hard.

Tim held his jacket over his head. Within one block from school, he was completely soaked.

Tim fought his way forward. But at times, the storm pushed him back. Tim grabbed hold of trees whenever he could.

"Stay low," he told himself. "Push and pull yourself from object to object."

Lightning flashed from a few blocks away. Thunder instantly rumbled. But the thunder was drowned out by the deafening roar of the tornado.

Tim checked his jacket thermometer. It read 54 degrees.

I sure am cold, he thought. I wonder what the **wind chill** is.

And he wrapped himself in his jacket.

Tim checked the sky. The huge funnel

Wind Chill

Strong winds blow away body heat. This makes it feel colder than the actual temperature. And this is called *wind chill*. Strong winds combined with water make it seem even colder.

continued to spin. Tim couldn't take his eyes off it. For a second, he felt calm and relaxed. Then a tree branch smacked him on the leg.

He saw that branches were being blown around like shredded newspaper. Tim moved a large limb out of his path. And he tried to keep moving.

The tornado now sounded like a train. It seemed to Tim that he was under a huge vacuum cleaner. It was sucking everything up, including him!

Wind slammed Tim against a tree. Tim grabbed it and held on with all his might. His body seemed to float in the air as the tree bent. For the first time, Tim was scared.

"Help!" he cried. "Don't break, tree! Please don't break!"

The tornado had turned a corner onto Tim's street. It was heading straight toward him!

Tim realized that he had made a mistake.

"I should have stayed at school!" he shouted at the howling wind.

He started thinking—

How far am I from school? Should I run back? What about home? I could grab Rainbow and run down to the storm cellar . . .

Lightning touched the ground across the street. Tim saw the streak hit the top branch of a tree. Its electricity surged through the tree and down the trunk. The whole tree lit up. And crackling thunder boomed.

Without another thought, Tim raced toward his house. "Rainbow! Rainbow!"

🌩 🌩 🌩

Meanwhile, Eric watched Sharon's broadcast on the TV at the back of the van. She warned viewers—

"If you are in this twister's path, seek shelter immediately. Get to the lowest floor of the house. The basement is best. Try to get as many walls between you and the storm as possible. The middle of a building with no outside walls or windows is also safer. Flying debris is very dangerous . . ."

Eric looked out the side window. The tornado kept traveling behind a series of houses and trees. Then it would show itself again.

Eric pointed his camera out the window. "This is going to be an incredible video!

"I've never gotten this close to a tornado before! Not even during my storm-chaser days."

The driver stopped when he saw the tornado at the end of the block. It was ripping up homes.

Eric felt helpless. "What if the whole neighborhood is destroyed?" he asked.

But there was nothing he could do. And he knew it.

"We gotta get outta here!" the driver declared.

Storm-Chaser Safaris

Remember the tornado chasers in the movie *Twister?* Tour groups can now chase storms in the middle of Tornado Alley. Right during peak thunderstorm season! The 10- to 14-day tours are offered between April and June.

In most cases, you have to be 18 years old to go. You get your own videotape of the storms at the end. For information, contact the following organizations:

- 🌩 Silver Lining Tours
- 🌩 Tornado Alley Safaris
- 🌩 Cloud 9 Tours

"Turn here," Eric said. And they sped toward the school and—they hoped—away from the storm.

Tim struggled on.

He came to Mr. Johnson's house. But Fang was nowhere in sight. Tim grabbed the metal fence. He held on like he would never let go.

All at once, the rain stopped. And everything seemed calm.

Suddenly, an explosion of light hit the sky. It lit up the area. A surge of electricity went up Tim's arm. It ran through his body. He stood frozen, with his hand stuck to the metal fence.

Tim looked up one last time. He saw the furious monster of a sky glare back at him. Then he passed out.

Chapter 8

Hot lights blared on Tim's head. He felt like he was burning up. He couldn't move. A cool, moist towel was draped on his forehead. Tim couldn't figure out who put it there. Or why.

Tim's mom whispered into his ear. "Tim, honey, can you hear me? Guess who's here?" she added. She was trying to pull Tim out of his state.

Then Tim heard another voice.

> **"There were no fatalities, thank goodness. The Elm Street subdivision was one of the worst-hit areas. Some homes were destroyed. But others were spared. The twister missed the middle school by just three blocks . . ."**

That voice was familiar.

Tim finally managed to open his eyes. TV cameras and lights crowded the room. So did a sea of people. Images flickered across the hospital room TV screen. They were pictures of Tim's broken neighborhood.

Tim tried to bring himself to full attention. But he was confused, weak, and groggy.

Eric Loffman noticed Tim stirring. "Do you think he's okay?" he asked Tim's mom.

She nodded and said, "I think so. Tim?"

Tim looked up. "Mom? Where am I? What happened?"

Lightning Strikes

Most lightning-strike victims are not struck directly. They usually get an electrical shock from a nearby lightning strike.

People report that the feeling of being hit by lightning is both strange and severe. Limbs may go numb. The chest hurts. And there is usually a terrible smell.

Electricity travels through the body. Victims have *entrance wounds* where they were hit. And *exit wounds* where the lightning left the body.

Many times, victims have short-term memory loss. Lightning victims are usually only knocked out for a short time. When they come to, they may not remember things clearly for the next several days. They may have blurred vision.

They may also have permanent nerve or muscle damage and other more severe problems.

A person directly struck by lightning can die. Many people who have been hit never totally recover.

Tim experienced a *Boston-fern burn pattern*. It is not common. But it can happen. This type of burn usually goes away in a few days. It does not need to be treated.

Metal, Water, and Lightning

It is unsafe to be near water or metal during a thunderstorm. Both of these *conduct* electricity. That means that electricity runs through them.

During a thunderstorm, you should stay away from wire fences, pipes, and rails. Stay away from water too. If you are outside, seek shelter in a building or car. The windows should be rolled up.

If you are outside and feel your hair stand on end, lightning may be about to strike. Find a low-lying area at once. Drop to your knees. And bend forward while putting your hands on your knees. Make yourself as small as possible. Do not lie flat on the ground.

If you are in the woods, seek shelter among a thick patch of small trees. Stay away from large, isolated trees. They may attract lightning.

Lynn, the anchorwoman on the TV, asked Eric a question.

"What about our friend Tim there? It looks like he's coming to."

Eric asked,

"Mrs. Skinner? May we speak to Tim?"

"Go ahead," Tim's mom replied.
Eric smiled at Tim and then spoke into a microphone.

"Tim Skinner is my friend and weather watcher. He was outside during this dangerous storm."

Tim suddenly noticed that he was on live TV! He tried to jump up out of his hospital bed. But he felt a tremendous aching feeling in his arm. He saw that his hand was totally wrapped in gauze.
Eric continued.

"Tim apparently ran home from school in the middle of the storm. And he was indirectly struck by lightning while holding onto a metal fence. Just seconds later, our camera crew drove by. And we alerted the paramedics . . ."

Tim felt a sharp pain go all the way up his arm. He noticed a fernlike burn around his upper arm and shoulder. Tim realized that he'd been hit by lightning there.
He tried to move his hand. But he couldn't. It was too painful.
Then he noticed that his foot was also wrapped in gauze. He wondered if he'd been hit by lightning there too.

"How are you, Tim?" Eric asked, holding out the microphone.

"Fine, I think." Tim squeaked. He was embarrassed by all the attention.

"Do you know what happened?"

"I think so. I did something I never should have done. I took off from school during the storm. I really wanted to see a tornado. And I wanted to protect my cat.

"As I ran down the street, I was knocked all over the place. The wind and the rain were really strong. Lightning was hitting everywhere. I grabbed a metal fence to brace myself against the storm. And that's all I remember."

Eric turned toward the TV camera. He spoke seriously—

"I am very happy to report that Tim is recovering. But let this be a lesson for all of you. Thunderstorms are very powerful. Lightning and tornadoes can severely hurt and kill.

"Tim was lucky. And we are all happy about that. But please don't copy what he did. Never venture out into these storms!"

Eric continued his live report.

"I'm also glad to report that this storm has passed through. Tomorrow looks like a much calmer day. That will give everyone in the Elm Street area and all of Wichita a chance to clean up.

"This is Eric Loffman reporting live at Mercy Hospital. Back to you, Lynn."

Injury and Death Statistics

Lightning kills about 100 Americans per year.
Tornadoes kill about 90 Americans per year.

Many more people are injured from lightning and tornadoes each year. The property damage caused by both is in the hundreds of millions of dollars.

"Thanks, Eric. And tell Tim that we're all very happy that he is recovering."

Tim smiled.

The TV lights in the room turned off. The cameraman switched off the monitor.

"Nice job, Eric," he said.

"Thanks."

Tim was awake and alert now. He looked around the room. There were his mom and Mr. D. And several of Tim's classmates were there. Even Greg was there!

Tim's eyes found Jill in the corner of the hospital room. She was smiling. And she held something in her hand.

Jill walked over and sat down next to Tim. She put her hand on his arm. And she spoke softly.

"I'm glad you're okay, Funnel Cloud Boy."

Tim laughed.

"I brought you something," Jill added. "This is so you don't have to go chasing tornadoes anymore."

Jill presented a plastic container. She gently shook it. And inside appeared a tiny, swirling tornado. The twister twirled around a miniature scene of the plains.

Tim stared at the swirling, safe tornado.

"I bet it's only an F0," Tim joked.

Jill smiled and glanced around the roomful of people. Then she quickly turned back to Tim and kissed him on the cheek.

Tim blushed.

And Tim's mom came over and hugged him.

Tornado Tubes

You can make tornado tubes at home.

You'll need

two 1-liter bottles

1"–2" section of hose

cloth tape

Fill one of the bottles ⅔ full with water. You may want to add a little glitter to the water for effect. Attach the hose to one bottle. Secure the hose with cloth tape. Put the other bottle upside down into the other end of the hose. Use cloth tape to secure the hose around both bottle tops.

Then turn the water-filled bottle upward. Shake vigorously in a circle. You've got your tornado!

The Most Destructive Tornadoes of All Time

The Great Tristate Tornado .

This is considered the worst tornado ever. It carved a path through Missouri, Illinois, and Indiana on March 18, 1925. Over 700 people were killed.

People had no idea it was coming. So they weren't properly protected.

> A tornado once stayed on the ground for 292 miles! This happened on May 26, 1917, between Illinois and Indiana.

Men search the rubble at Griffin, Indiana on March 23, 1925.

The Super Outbreak

Another famous tornado took place April 3 and April 4, 1974. The Super Outbreak produced 148 tornadoes in a 13-state area east of the Mississippi.

At least six of the tornadoes had winds over 261 mph.

More than 300 people died. And more than 6,000 were injured.

Jarrell, Texas

A tornado outbreak happened in Jarrell, Texas, on May 27, 1997. It will be remembered as one of the worst tornado outbreaks ever.

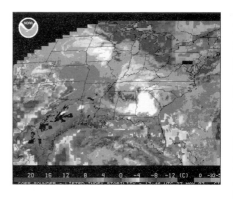

There were eight twisters that day. And there were 49 tornado warnings.

Damage surveys rated the Jarrell tornado as an F5. Its winds were estimated at 260 mph.

The tornado stayed on the ground for over six miles. Twenty-seven people died in less than ten minutes.

Andover, Kansas

The most famous tornado took place in Andover, Kansas. It occurred April 26, 1991.

It was rated an F5 on the Fujita Scale. Damage indicated winds of 261–318 mph. In all, 17 people died.

This tornado has been described as the most photographed tornado event of all time.

Tornado Safety

Creating a tornado-safety plan for home is a smart idea. Keep these facts and tips in mind.

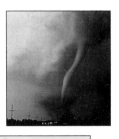

- Tornadoes occur most often in April, May, and June. But they can develop at any time of year.

- Most tornadoes occur in mid-afternoon or early evening. But they can happen at any time. Plan ahead. Know where to go if a tornado approaches.

- Small rooms near the center of a building are safer in a tornado. For example, go to a closet or a bathroom. Stay away from exterior walls.

- Storm cellars and basements offer greater tornado protection. If neither is available, go the lowest part of the building.

- If a tornado approaches at night, it may be hidden. Listen for a loud roar similar to a train. If you hear this, take shelter immediately.

- Trying to flee from a tornado in a car can be very dangerous. A ditch or a ravine offers the best protection. This is also true if you live in a mobile home. If possible, get out of the mobile home and into a ditch or ravine.

- If it is hailing, seek appropriate shelter from a possible tornado. Remain protected for up to 30 minutes after the hail has stopped.

- Opening a window in a house during a tornado does not necessarily reduce damage.

Glossary

air mass a large body of air. The same conditions of **humidity** and temperature are present at nearly all levels.

anemometer an instrument that measures wind speed

barometer an instrument that measures air pressure. It is often used to predict oncoming storms.

cloud chart chart or poster that depicts basic cloud types. The chart includes descriptions, atmospheric level, and type of weather to be expected.

cold front caused by cold air wedging underneath a warm air mass

cumulonimbus a dense, vertical cloud. Often has an anvil shape at the top. Frequently brings thunderstorms and hail.

cumulus a flat-based cloud with a bulging upper part. Usually brings fair weather. Can become a larger cloud that may bring stormy weather.

Doppler radar highly sensitive radar. It can measure the movement of objects and rotation. It can also measure **precipitation.**

downdraft the area of a storm where the air or precipitation is falling

dry line a boundary that separates moist and dry air masses. Typically lies on a north-south line. The line separates Gulf of Mexico moisture to the east and dry desert air from the west.

Fujita Scale a scale that rates tornado intensity by surveying damage

funnel cloud	a rotating column of air. It descends from a cloud but does not touch the ground.
Gulf of Mexico	a large body of water. It is directly south of the southeastern United States. It is warm and often sends moisture into the U.S. This fuels thunderstorms.
hail	particles of ice falling from a cumulonimbus cloud
ham radio	an amateur radio system. It is used by spotters and chasers for relaying important weather-related information.
humidity	the degree of moisture in the air
hygrometer	an instrument for measuring the air's water vapor or humidity
lightning rod	a metal rod placed high on a building. It helps divert lightning away from the structure.
mammatus cloud	part of a cumulonimbus cloud. It looks like pouches hanging from the bottom of the cloud. It does not produce severe weather but can indicate strong winds.
maximum/minimum thermometer	a thermometer that automatically measures the high and low temperatures during a 24-hour period
mesocyclone	intense rotating winds in the lower part of a thunderstorm. Usually brings hail, damaging winds, or tornadoes.
meteorologist	a person who studies the atmosphere and its interaction with the earth's surface
precipitation	any form of water—liquid or solid—that falls from the atmosphere and reaches the ground

radar	a device that bounces radio waves off an object. It measures the distance and keeps track of its movements. Often associated with rainfall.
rain-free base	a part of a large thunderstorm with no visible precipitation beneath it. This part of the storm often produces tornadoes.
rain gauge	a device for measuring rainfall amounts
rotation	act of spinning
satellite loop	a loop showing the current satellite information of a specific area
satellite picture	a photograph of earth from a satellite in orbit. It can show cloud, wind, and precipitation patterns.
supercell storm	a long-lived thunderstorm with a persistent rotating updraft. It produces a high percentage of violent tornadoes, large hail, and damaging winds.
thunderstorm	a vigorous storm forming from a cumulonimbus cloud. It is accompanied by thunder, lightning, and heavy rain. Hail can also occur. Tornadoes can too.
tornado	an intense rotating funnel of air that descends from a cumulonimbus cloud and touches the ground
Tornado Alley	an area of the Great Plains and east-central United States where the highest level of tornado activity occurs
tornado warning	indicates that a tornado has been reported on the ground. Immediate danger exists. People should take action quickly to save lives.

tornado watch	identifies a large area where tornadoes are possible
updraft	the area of a storm where the air is rising upward
updrafting	air rising upward
weather radio	a special radio that broadcasts weather-related information 24 hours a day
weather watcher	a person who reports the daily weather to the local TV station
wind chill	the cooling effect of a combination of temperature and wind
wind sock	a device used to determine the direction of the wind. Often seen at airports and on boat docks.
wind vane	an instrument used to determine wind direction

Index